Oceans
and Seas

KINGFISHER

Published in 2011 by Kingfisher
This edition published in 2013 by Kingfisher
an imprint of Macmillan Children's Books
a division of Macmillan Publishers Limited
20 New Wharf Road, London N1 9RR
Basingstoke and Oxford
Associated companies throughout the world
www.panmacmillan.com

ISBN 978-0-7534-3727-8

First published as *Kingfisher Young Knowledge: Oceans and Seas* in 2007
Additional material produced for Macmillan Children's Books by Discovery Books Ltd

Copyright © Macmillan Children's Books 2011

1 3 5 7 9 8 6 4 2
1SPL/0713/WKT/UTD/128MA

A CIP catalogue record for this book is available from the British Library.

Printed in China

Note to readers: the website addresses listed in this book are correct at the time of going to print.
However, due to the ever-changing nature of the internet, website addresses and content can
change. Websites can contain links that are unsuitable for children. The publisher cannot be held
responsible for changes in website addresses or content, or for information obtained through
a third party. We strongly advise that internet searches be supervised by an adult.

Acknowledgements
The publisher would like to thank the following for permission to reproduce their material. Every care has been taken
to trace copyright holders. However, if there have been unintentional omissions or failure to trace copyright holders,
we apologise and will, if informed, endeavour to make corrections in any future edition.
b = bottom, *c* = centre, *l* = left, *t* = top, *r* = right

Photographs: *cover* Shutterstock Images/Brian J Abela; *pages* 1 Getty; 2–3 Getty; 4–5 Corbis; 6 Getty; 7*tr* National
Geographic Image Collection (NGIC); 7*cl* Nature Picture Library; 7*br* Minden Pictures/Frank Lane Picture Agency;
8–9 Corbis; 9*tl* Alamy; 9*b* Corbis; 11*b* Corbis; 12–13 Getty; 13*tl* Oxford Scientific Films (OSF); 13*cl* OSF; 13*br* Corbis;
14 Press Association, London; 15 Corbis; 15*t* Corbis; 16–17 Getty; 16*b* Science Photo Library (SPL); 17*t* OSF; 18–19
Ardea; 19*tl* NGIC; 19*br* Ardea; 20 Getty; 21 Getty; 21*b* Nature Picture Library 22–23 Corbis; 22*bl* Corbis; 23*tl* Getty;
24–25 NGIC; 26*bl* Nature Picture Library; 27*tl* Nature Picture Library; 27*cr* Nature Picture Library; 27*b* Nature Picture
Library; 28–29 Corbis; 28*bl* Getty; 30*b* Getty; 31 Ardea; 31*bl* Ardea; 32*bl* Corbis; 33*t* Minden Pictures/Frank Lane
Picture Agency; 33*b* Image Quest 3D; 34–35 Getty; 34*bl* Image Quest 3D; 35*tl* Nature Picture Library; 36–37 Corbis;
36*bl* SPL; 37*tr* SPL; 38 Corbis; 39 Getty; 40*bl* Getty; 40–41 Getty; 41*t* Getty; 48*t* Shutterstock Images/Jan Daly;
48*b* Shutterstock Images/Alberto Loyo; 49*l* Shutterstock Images/P. Borowka; 49*r* Shutterstock Images/Leksele;
52*l* Shutterstock Images/R-studio; 52*r* Shutterstock Images/Christian Wilkinson; 53*t* Shutterstock
Images/tonobalaguerf; 53*b* Shutterstock Images/magicinfoto; 56 Corbis

Commissioned photography on pages 42–47 by Andy Crawford
Thank you to models Lewis Manu and Rebecca Roper

Oceans
and Seas

Nicola Davies

KINGFISHER

Contents

Planet ocean

Only one-third of the Earth is dry land, so our planet looks blue when seen from space. The rest of the planet is ocean, and there is life in every part of it!

an ocean is a large sea

Sunlit surface

The ocean's surface is full of tiny plants and animals called plankton, which are eaten by bigger creatures, such as these jellyfish.

Keeping hidden

Many animals, like this octopus, prefer the deeper water of the middle ocean. Here they can hide from predators and be safe from storms.

Deep and dark

The deepest waters are totally dark and cold. Food is hard to find, so animals here have big mouths, to eat anything!

Salty sea

All seas and oceans are salty, with about 35 grams of salt in every kilogram of water. That is as salty as one large spoonful of salt in half a bucket of water!

Saltiest sea

The Dead Sea in Asia is so salty that when its water is turned to vapour by the sun, the salt is left behind in hard white lumps.

Salty sources

Volcanic hot spots on land and on the sea floor add salt to seawater when they release hot gases and molten rock. Rivers wash salt from the land into the seas and oceans.

Grains of salt

Some of the salt we put on our food comes from the sea. Sea salt is broken up into small pieces so we can sprinkle it on our dinner.

Undersea landscape

Hidden under the sea is a world of high mountains, wide plains and deep valleys – a whole landscape as interesting and varied as the one on dry land!

Flattest and deepest

Almost half of the deep ocean floor is made up of a large, flat area called the abyssal (deep) plain. Even deeper are the ocean trenches, which plunge 10,000 metres below the surface.

Mountaintop islands

When volcanoes form on the sea floor, they grow into mountains. These can get so tall that they stick out of the sea and make islands.

Black smokers

Deep seawater is usually very cold, but at volcanic spots called black smokers, water three times hotter than boiling gushes through cracks in the sea floor.

Tides and waves

Seawater is always moving. It is stirred by the heat of the sun and the cold of the ice at the North and South Poles, pushed by winds, and pulled by the sun and the movement of the moon.

Windy waves

When wind blows over water, it makes waves. Strong winds blowing for a long time make the biggest waves, which can be up to 34 metres high!

Tide out, tide in

The moon pulls water towards it as it goes around the Earth, making the seas and oceans bulge away from the coasts. This movement causes tides. Most tides happen twice a day – the sea moves away from the shore (tide out) and back again (tide in).

tide out

tide in

Eating land

In some places waves wash away beaches and cliffs, changing the shape of the coastline in just a few days.

14 Weather-making sea

The oceans make weather by warming or cooling the air over them, which creates winds and clouds. Ocean currents carry warmth and cold around the planet.

Hooray for rain!
Clouds from the Indian Ocean bring heavy rains to Asia and Africa. Without the rains, crops would not grow.

Hurricane!

Above warm, tropical seas air masses can sometimes develop into giant, spinning storms called hurricanes. These storms can move inland and cause enormous damage, destroying whole towns!

El Niño

Every few years a warm current called El Niño sweeps along the west coast of South America, causing extreme weather across the world – devastating storms, droughts, even heavy snow!

Living history

Life on Earth began in the sea, billions of years before there was life on land. Some of those early life forms are alive in the sea today!

First life on Earth?

Stromatolites are mounds of millions of tiny creatures. They look just like stromatolites from 3 billion years ago.

Living fossils

The coelacanth is a fish that was only known to us from million-year-old fossils, until in 1938 a living fish was caught by a fisherman.

Unchanged habits

Each year, horseshoe crabs surface from deep water to lay their eggs on sandy beaches, just as they have for 400 million years!

Fish rule

There are more than 20,000 different kinds of fish in all shapes and sizes, and most of them live in the oceans and seas.

Ocean hunters

Big fish, such as this blue shark, are the predators of the sea. Most sharks hunt animals for food, and can swim really fast so they can catch their dinner.

Fish or seaweed?

The leafy sea dragon has great camouflage. It looks so much like seaweed that it can hide among the plants and not be seen by other fish that might want to eat it.

Safety in numbers

In a shoal of fish there is a greater chance of spotting danger (lots of eyes), and a smaller chance of being eaten (lots of other fish could be eaten instead)!

Ocean mammals

Sea mammals are shaped for swimming. They have smooth, streamlined bodies that can slip through the water, and they can hold their breath for a long time when they dive.

Sea flyers

Sea lions use their webbed front feet to row them along – fast! It is like underwater flying, and it makes catching fish easy!

Legless dolphins

Dolphins do not have back legs at all! They swim by beating their tails up and down, and steer with paddle-shaped feet called flippers.

Sea cows

Dugongs also use their tails and flippers for swimming. These large, heavy animals graze on plants called seagrasses, so their other name is 'sea cow'.

Super sea birds

Sea birds are tough! They fly hundreds or thousands of kilometres every year to find food at sea. They survive storms and rough seas, and still find their way back to land to nest. Phew!

All puffed up
Male frigatebirds puff up their bright red chests like balloons to impress female birds and find mates to nest with.

Tiny traveller

The tiny Arctic tern travels 24,000 kilometres every year, from the Arctic Ocean to the Antarctic Ocean.

Long wings

Huge wingspans of up to 3.5 metres carry albatrosses over the stormiest oceans in search of food.

Diving for dinner

Puffins dive for food, using their wings underwater like paddles. They catch small fish to feed to their chicks on land.

Who eats whom?

Ocean life, just like life on land, depends on plants. Animals that eat plants are called herbivores. The herbivores are eaten by carnivores, or meat eaters. This is called a food chain.

Big mouth, short chain!
The whale shark is the world's biggest fish (up to 15 metres long)! Its food chain is very short because it feeds on the smallest animals and plants in the sea – plankton.

killer whale

eats

porpoise

eats

cod

eats

herring

eats

zoo-plankton

eats

phyto-plankton

Big mouth, long chain

Killer whales need big food – they cannot eat the tiny plankton. There are five links in the food chain between killer whales and the smallest plants in the ocean, phyto-plankton.

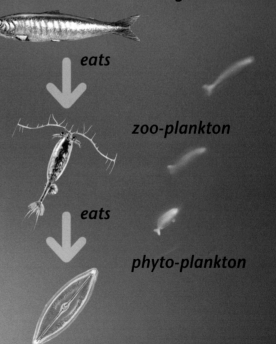

Coral reef

In tropical seas, where the water is warm and clear, corals grow like forests of small pink, yellow and white trees. They are full of colourful fish, and many other kinds of life.

Clever clowns!

Little clown fish can hide from danger amongst the stinging tentacles of big anemones because anemones never sting their own clown fish!

Super slug
The sea slug's bright colours are a warning to predators that it has a sting in its orange skin!

Plant-like corals
Corals look like plants, but they are really animals with soft bodies protected by a hard, stony skeleton. They are related to anemones.

Kelp jungles

All over the world, where the sea is cool and the coastline is rocky, there are underwater jungles of huge seaweeds called kelps.

Jungle eaters

Sea urchins eat kelp and, although they are small, they can munch their way through a forest of seaweed.

... and jungle savers

Luckily, many animals eat sea urchins.
Seals, dogfish, lobsters and sea otters,
such as this one floating in a kelp forest
off the west coast of America, love to
snack on the spiky animals.

Frozen feast

Antarctica is the huge frozen land around the South Pole. It looks like an icy desert, but the ocean around it is full of fish, birds, seals and whales.

Penguin crowds

Seven kinds of penguins live in the Antarctic but these adelies are the most common. There can be five million of them in one nesting area!

Whale schools

Humpbacked whales, as well as 14 other kinds of whale and dolphin, travel to the Antarctic every summer just to feed.

... and here is what they eat...

Krill! These shrimp-like animals are not big, just 4 centimetres long, but there are a lot of them. A single swarm can cover 45,000 football pitches and weigh 2 million tonnes!

Deep oceans

In the deepest parts of the ocean, it is always cold and completely dark. The pressure of water would squash you flat, yet even here there is life.

Deepest divers

Sperm whales dive 300 to 3,000 metres down to feed on giant squid. They can hold their breath for almost an hour!

Silver camouflage

Hatchet fish stay hidden in deep water by having shiny skin that matches the gleam of the surface far above.

Shine a light

Some animals make their own light from chemicals in their bodies, so they can find each other in the dark or scare off predators.

Ocean **mysteries**

Humans have only just begun to explore life in the sea. There is so much we do not know about some of the biggest and most beautiful marine animals.

Giant mystery...
The ocean sun fish or mola mola weighs up to 2,000 kilograms and eats plankton, but that is almost all we know about this huge fish.

...and mysterious giant

Manta rays can be six metres across but, like the mola mola, all we know about them is that they swim the oceans eating plankton.

Bye-bye baby!

Baby turtles hatch on sandy beaches then disappear out to sea. We do not know what they do next, only that they return many years later to breed and lay their eggs.

Studying the sea

The ocean is not our home – we cannot breathe underwater and we are poor swimmers. However, there are still ways of finding out about the sea.

Follow that seal!
This fur seal has a radio tag attached to its back. It sends signals telling scientists where the seal goes and how deep it dives.

Down to the bottom

Tough little submersibles
can carry cameras and
other equipment to the
deepest ocean to find
out what goes on there.

Underwater history

Ancient shipwrecks can lie
undisturbed on the sea bed
for thousands of years.
Modern scuba (breathing)
gear helps divers to explore
them and discover more
about human history.

All fished out

For thousands of years, humans have caught fish to eat. In the past, people used simple nets and sailing boats. But now we use motor boats and huge nylon nets – the fish do not stand a chance.

Useless slaughter

Nets catch anything. Every year, millions of dolphins, turtles, sharks, mola molas and birds die in fishing nets meant to catch something else.

Fishing for trouble

People have become too good at fishing. There are now fewer and fewer fish left to catch. Some fish, such as cod, have almost disappeared!

What a waste!

All over the world, people use oceans and seas as dustbins for all kinds of rubbish that kills marine life, but it does not have to be this way.

Stop the spill

If ships carrying oil were made extra strong, oil would not spill so easily when the ships crash.

Safe sewage

Sewage can be made safe enough to spread on farmland, not just dumped into the sea.

Perfect plastic

Plastic rubbish is ugly, and can trap and harm marine animals. This waste can be used again or made so that it breaks down naturally.

Tasty sea slug

You will need
- Block of marzipan
- Plate
- Food colouring and brush
- Coloured sweets

A bitter taste
Sea slugs are not eaten by anything in the sea – they taste really horrible! However, here is a sea slug that is tasty to eat.

1

To make the slug's long body, roll the marzipan between your hands into a sausage shape. Then put the shape on to a plate.

2

Many sea slugs have frills. Use your fingers to press down along the bottom edges of the body to make a frill along each side.

3

Dip your paintbrush into some food colouring and paint the frills. The frills can be any colour. Paint dots of colour down the slug's back.

4

Sea slugs can be very bright. Decorate the slug's body with coloured sweets. Use two sweets as antennae on the slug's head.

Making waves

Wind-power

Wind blowing across the sea makes waves. The stronger the wind blows, the bigger the waves are. Find out how in this project.

You will need
- Large, clear glass bowl
- Water
- Blue food colouring
- Spoon

Fill the bowl half-full with water and add a few drops of blue food colouring. Stir the water to mix.

2 Blow across the surface of the water – this is like wind blowing across the sea. Blow hard and you will see large waves.

Paper-plate fish

Shiny scales

Fish come in all sizes, shapes and colours. Use different colours of shiny paper to make a variety of paper-plate fish.

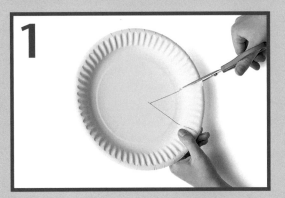

Draw a triangle on the plate and cut it out to make a mouth. Glue the triangle piece on to the body, opposite the mouth, to make a tail.

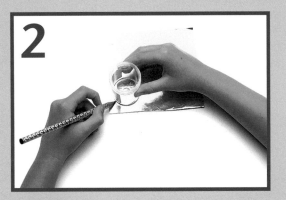

Using a pencil, draw around a round bottle cap and make 30 circles on the sheets of shiny paper and foil. Then cut them out.

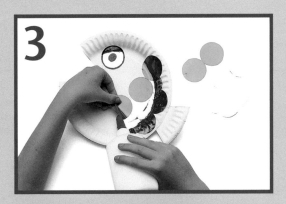

Glue on a silver circle above the mouth and draw a black dot in the centre to make the eye. Then stick the other circles on to the body.

Sandy starfish

Many arms, but no legs!
Most starfish have five arms, but some have more than 50 arms! They use them to move around and to catch prey.

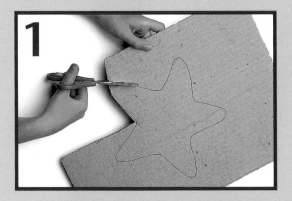

Draw a starfish shape on to the cardboard and cut it out. Copy the starfish shape from this page.

You will need
- Thick cardboard
- Pencil
- Scissors
- Glue and glue brush
- Teaspoon
- Orange and pink coloured sand

Draw a line about 1 centimetre around the inside of the starfish, following the starfish shape. Spread glue over the inner starfish shape.

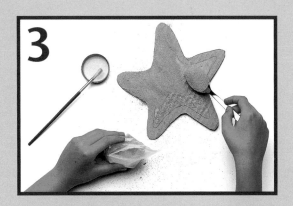

Use the spoon to sprinkle on the orange sand. Press down the sand and leave to dry. Do the same with pink sand on the rim of the starfish.

Jolly jellyfish

Many tentacles

Jellyfish use their tentacles to gather food as they swim. There are over 200 types of jellyfish and some have tentacles that are 30 metres long!

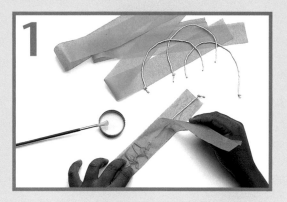

1

Glue each piece of string down the middle of four strips of tissue paper, from top to middle. Fold up the remaining paper to cover the string.

You will need
- Glue and glue brush
- 4 pieces of string, 20cm long
- Green tissue paper cut into 5 strips, 40cm long
- Scissors
- Coloured paper plate
- Sticky tape
- Shiny paper

2

Cut the plate in half. Place each green tissue tentacle on to the back of the plate half and stick each one down with sticky tape.

3

Glue the fifth tissue paper strip along the curve of the plate half. Then cut out circles of shiny paper and decorate the jellyfish body.

Seascape

You will need

- Glue and glue brush
- Green tissue paper, cut into strips
- Large piece of hard blue card
- Sand
- Pen or pencil
- Shiny paper
- Scissors

All together

Here, you can create an underwater landscape to show the crafts you have made in this book.

1

Glue the tissue paper on to the card and spread glue over the bottom of the card. Pour sand over the glue and pat it down.

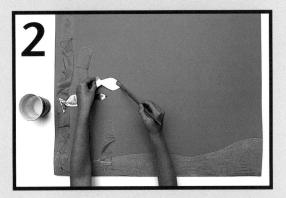

2

Draw fish on to the shiny paper. Cut them out and stick them onto the card. You can also add any other sea animals you have made.

Use different-coloured paper, foil and sand to make more sea creatures for your seascape.

Glossary

Abyssal plain – a large, flat area of land deep on the sea floor

Billion – 1,000 million, written like this: 1,000,000,000

Camouflage – a shape, colour or pattern that helps to hide an animal

Carnivore – a meat-eating animal

Coast – the shore, where sea and land meet

Current – the movement of seawater within a sea or ocean

Fossil – the remains of ancient animals or plants that have gradually turned into rock

Herbivore – a plant-eating animal

Marine animal – an animal that lives in or on the sea

Nylon – tough, synthetic thread

Predator – an animal that hunts and eats other animals

Pressure – the weight of water in the ocean

Radio tag – a device which sends out invisible signals that travel long distances

School – a group of whales

Sewage – body waste that you flush down the toilet

Shoal – a group of one kind of fish

Streamlined – having a smooth body shape that moves easily though the water

Submersible – a machine that can dive underwater

Swarm – a large group of small animals

Tentacles – long, bendy parts of an animal, used for gripping, feeling or moving

Trenches – long, narrow, underwater valleys, usually formed next to islands or mountains

Vapour – a mist or gas given off when something is heated

Volcanic – describes anything to do with volcanoes

Webbed – describes toes that are joined together by a flap of skin

Wingspan – the distance between a bird's wingtips

Zoo-plankton – a type of plankton that is an animal, not a plant

This book includes material that would be particularly useful in helping to teach children aged 7–11. It covers many elements of the English and Science curricula, especially the science topics of habitats, life cycles, food chains and the Earth. It could also be useful in helping to teach elements of geography themes such as seas, coasts, map skills and climate.

Extension activities

Writing
Each double-page information spread has a title, introduction, and three paragraphs of text, each with its own sub-heading. Pages 12 and 13 explain the tides. Write a report, poem or animal diary showing how the coast is different when the tide is in and out.

There is information on food chains on pages 7, 18–19, 24–25, 27, 28–29, 31 and 32. Write a short story or poem that follows a food chain from the smallest creature to the final predator.

Speaking and listening
On a large piece of paper, draw and colour a fish of your own design. Write a description including such things as its habitat, geographic location, predators and prey, defences and life cycle. Give a short talk about your fish, using your picture as a visual aid.

Pages 34–35 show some ocean mysteries. Make up a two-minute talk explaining one of them. You can use information from this book as well as your imagination.

Science
There is background on habitats on pages 6 and 7, 10, 11, 22, 23, 26, 27, 28, 29, 30, 31, 32, 36, 37, 38 and 39. For background on the Earth and its environment see pages 6, 8, 9, 10, 11, 12, 13, 14, 15, 38, 39, 40 and 41.

Page 8 explains how the sea is salty. Dissolve some salt in water, then leave the container in a warm place until the water evaporates. What is left behind?

Pages 40–41 explain about rubbish. Make a list of materials that harm the sea, and suggest alternatives that would do less damage.

Cross-curricular links
Art: Create a picture that shows the three layers under the sea as described on page 7.

Geography: Pages 10–11 describe the undersea landscape. Draw a map of the bottom of a sea, using a key to show mountains, volcanoes, plains and valleys.

Pages 14–15 and 23 mention different parts of the world. Find them in an atlas. Which countries might the Arctic tern cross on its journey?

Using the projects
Children can follow or adapt these projects at home. Here are some ideas for extending them:

Page 42: Use foods to make models of other animals from this book.

Page 43: Use a clear glass baking pan to study wave activity. Wearing safety glasses, blow, tilt the pan in different directions and otherwise disturb the water. Watch from the sides as well as above. Float a small cork to see how different waves move it.

Page 43: Use modelling clay to design and make a boat that will float even when you blow waves at it.

Page 44: Using the information about camouflage on pages 19 and 32, make a fish with patterns and colour to blend in with its surroundings. On page 27 is information on the sea slug. Draw and paint a creature that is coloured to warn off predators.

Page 45: Make a sea bed from papier maché for your starfish to hide in.

Page 46: Make a jellyfish mobile, using a wire coat hanger and cotton thread.

Page 47: Make a 3-D seascape from papier maché in a shoebox. Add sea creatures made of card and painted.

Did you know?

- Over two-thirds of the Earth's surface is covered by water.

- The average depth of the ocean is more than 4 kilometres.

- The world's oceans contain around 20 million tonnes of gold.

- Ninety per cent of all volcanic activity occurs in the oceans.

- The blue whale is the largest animal in the ocean. It's as long as three buses!

- A tsunami is a huge ocean wave produced by an underwater earthquake.

- The deepest part of any ocean is the Marianas Trench, which reaches a depth of 11,000 metres below sea level.

- The world's largest fish is the whale shark. It can grow up to 15 metres long.

- The fastest fish in the sea is the sailfish. It can swim at speeds of up to 110 kilometres per hour.

- Every year, the weight of all the rubbish dumped in the sea is three times more than the weight of all the fish caught by fishermen.

- The grey whale migrates 16,000 kilometres each year, the furthest distance of any mammal.

- Sea kelp can grow up to 30 metres long.

- The largest ocean in the world is the Pacific. The smallest is the Arctic.

- More people have been in space than have visited the deepest parts of the ocean.

- The oceans contain 99 per cent of the living space on the planet.

- The ocean is blue because it reflects blue light rays from the sun.

- There is no marine life in the Dead Sea. It is so salty that plants and fish cannot live there.

Oceans and seas quiz

The answers to these questions can all be found by looking back through the book. See how many you get right. You can check your answers on page 56.

1) How many different kinds of fish are there?
   A – 20
   B – 200
   C – 20,000

2) How large is the wingspan of the albatross?
   A – 3.5 metres
   B – 6 metres
   C – 10 metres

3) How far does the Arctic tern travel every year?
   A – 10,000 kilometres
   B – 24,000 kilometres
   C – 36,000 kilometres

4) What do whale sharks eat?
   A – Plankton
   B – Birds
   C – People

5) Where do clown fish hide from danger?
   A – In a clam shell
   B – Under a rock
   C – In the tentacles of anemones

6) Which sea has the saltiest water?
   A – The Red Sea
   B – The Dead Sea
   C – The Caspian Sea

7) What is the other name for a dugong?
   A – Sea cow
   B – Sea pig
   C – Sea elephant

8) How do male frigatebirds impress females?
   A – They sing a song
   B – They puff out their chests
   C – They do a dance

9) How many kinds of penguin live in the Antarctic?
   A – 1
   B – 17
   C – 7

10) For how long can sperm whales hold their breath underwater?
    A – 60 seconds
    B – 1 hour
    C – 6 hours

11) What is a group of fish called?
    A – A shoal
    B – A gang
    C – A squad

12) What is El Niño?
    A – A type of fish
    B – A warm current
    C – A Spanish president

Books to read

Discover More: Ocean and Sea by Steve Parker, Scholastic, 2012

Explorers: Oceans and Seas by Stephen Savage, Kingfisher, 2010

Life Cycles: Ocean by Sean Callery, Kingfisher, 2011

Navigators: Oceans and Seas by Margaret Hynes, Kingfisher, 2010

On the Sea Bed by John Woodward, Franklin Watts, 2009

Weird Ocean, Kingfisher, 2010

Places to visit

Birmingham Sea Life Centre
www.sealife.co.uk
Embark on an underwater adventure where you can see turtles, sharks, clown fish and lots of other sea creatures.

Bristol Zoo
www.bristolzoo.org.uk
Bristol zoo has a number of sea life attractions including a penguin and seal enclosure, as well as a tropical aquarium.

Bluereef Aquarium
www.bluereefaquarium.co.uk
The Bluereef aquarium in Cornwall has over 40 live displays with everything from lobsters to sharks. They also run workshops and special tours to help children learn about underwater life.

Hunstanton Sea Life Sanctuary
www.sealsanctuary.co.uk
Hunstanton sea life sanctuary in Norfolk is home to otters, penguins and seals. It also has a large aquarium with a variety of tropical fish.

Websites

BBC Animals
www.bbc.co.uk/nature/animals
The BBC Animals website has a wealth of information on underwater creatures. It also has video footage of each animal from BBC programmes.

National Geographic
http://kids.nationalgeographic.co.uk/kids/activities/new/ocean/
This site has photographs, videos and games about the ocean and its wildlife.

The Marine Life Information Network
www.marlin.ac.uk
This website has a special section aimed at children with information on British sea life, quizzes, fun facts and virtual tours.

Hebridean Whale and Dolphin Trust
www.whaledolphintrust.co.uk
On this website you can find out all about whales and dolphins, with a wide selection of accompanying photographs.

Oceans and seas
quiz answers

1) C   7) A
2) A   8) B
3) B   9) C
4) A   10) B
5) C   11) A
6) B   12) B